D0127349

Goldilocks
and the Three Bears

Written by Nick Page
Illustrated by Clare Fennell

make
believe
ideas

In a house in the woods (who knows where?),
live Ma and Pa and Mary Bear.
While their porridge cools in the morning air,
they fetch some cream from the dairy.
Oh, bears, beware! Oh, bears, beware!
Beware of girls with golden hair!

Goldilocks with long, fair hair
finds the house – there's no one there –
and walks straight in – she doesn't care!
She doesn't find it scary.
**Oh, bears, beware! Oh, bears, beware!
Beware of girls with golden hair!**

She sees the porridge, all prepared.
"Too hot! Too cold!" the girl declares.
But one's just right, and then and there,
she takes the one for Mary.
Oh, bears, beware! Oh, bears, beware!
Beware of girls with golden hair!

And then she tries out all the chairs.

"Too hard! Too soft!" the girl despairs.

She squeezes into Mary's chair
and breaks it! How contrary!

Oh!

Oh, bears, beware! Oh, bears, beware!
Beware of girls with golden hair!

And now she makes her way upstairs
to try the beds of those three bears.

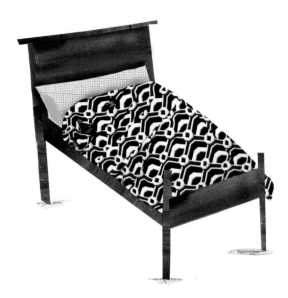

"Too high! Too low!" But over there –
the bed of little Mary.

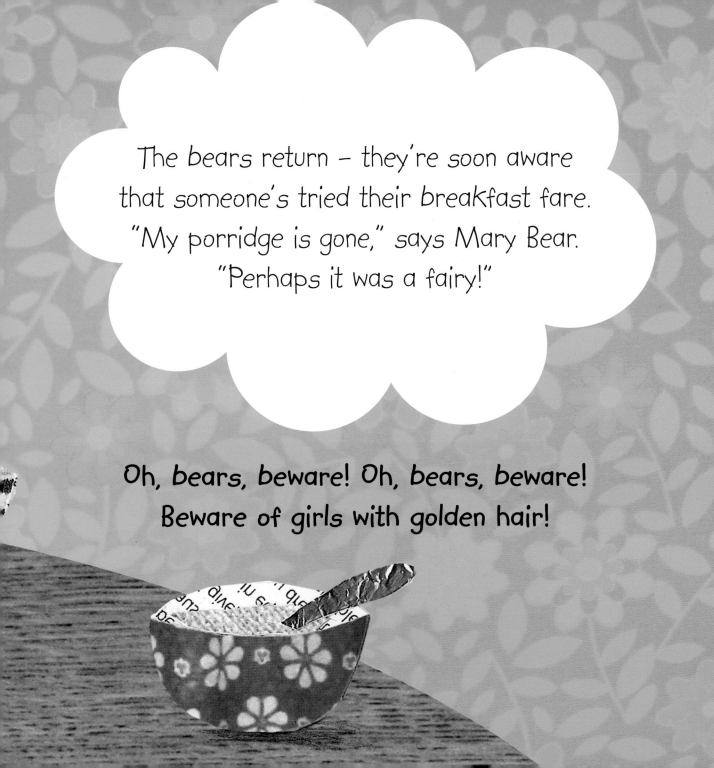

The bears return – they're soon aware
that someone's tried their breakfast fare.
"My porridge is gone," says Mary Bear.
"Perhaps it was a fairy!"

Oh, bears, beware! Oh, bears, beware!
Beware of girls with golden hair!

And then they see the broken chair,
with bits of wood spread everywhere.
It's ruined, quite beyond repair.

"I loved that chair," says Mary.

Oh, bears, beware! Oh, bears, beware!
Beware of girls with golden hair!

They hear a sound, and creep upstairs.
"Who's there?" says Pa. "Come out, who dares!"
In Mary's bed – oh, how they stare:
a girl, all golden-hairy!

Zzzzzzz!

Oh, bears, beware! Oh, bears, beware!
Beware of girls with golden hair!

"You porridge thief!" shouts Mommy Bear,
which gives the girl a dreadful scare!
She runs so fast away from there,
from Ma and Pa and Mary!

Oh, bears, beware! Oh, bears, beware!
Beware of girls with golden hair!

A word to small girls everywhere:
don't try the bed or break the chair,
and never, ever, dare to share
the porridge of little Mary!

Oh, bears, beware! Oh, bears, beware!
Beware of girls with golden hair!